Poisonous
Animals

Emily Bone

Illustrated by Paul Parker and Becka Moor

Designed by Alice Reese

Poisonous animals consultant: Dr. Naomi Ewald
Reading consultant: Alison Kelly

Contents

Deadly creatures

Poisonous animals have a liquid inside them that can kill or harm other animals.

Some animals use the liquid to kill food to eat. Others use it to stop animals from eating them.

This giant silkworm moth caterpillar is covered in poisonous spines.

Venom and poison

Different animals pass on their poison in different ways.

Some animals have a poisonous liquid, called venom. They inject the venom into animals by biting, scratching or stinging them.

This scorpion is injecting venom into a locust using the stinging tube on the end of its tail.

4

Other animals have poison in their bodies.
If an animal touches or eats any parts,
it will become very ill.

This is a fire salamander. Its skin is
filled with poison.

Snake attack

Some snakes have sharp, hollow teeth, called fangs.

This is a
puff adder.

You can see the
pointed fangs at
the front of the
snake's mouth.

Snakes inject venom through their fangs to catch animals to eat.

A bushmaster snake hunts for food by lying very still in some leaves.

A rat runs past. The bushmaster grabs the rat in its mouth and bites it.

Venom in the fangs flows into the rat. The rat dies, then the snake eats it.

Spitting cobras shoot venom in the eyes of attackers to blind them.

Scary spiders

Spiders have fangs to inject venom, too. The venom helps them to eat food.

A black widow spider builds a web using sticky silk. A moth flies into the web.

The moth sticks to the web. The spider wraps the moth in silk to keep it still.

The spider bites the moth. Venom shoots inside the moth's body.

The venom turns the moth's insides to liquid and the spider sucks them out.

Some spiders don't build webs.

This is a jumping spider. It has pounced on this fly and is biting it.

Venom in the spider's fangs will make the fly stay very still. Then, the spider will eat it.

A deadly bite

Komodo dragons are big lizards. They have venom in their spit that they use to kill animals for food.

This komodo dragon is flicking out its tongue to taste smells in the air.

The smells tell it when an animal, such as a deer, is nearby.

When a komodo dragon finds a deer, it hides in nearby bushes.

It waits for the deer to walk very near. Then, it charges at the deer and bites it.

Venom in the komodo dragon's spit flows into the deer. The deer dies.

The komodo dragon eats the deer. Other dragons come and eat the deer, too.

11

Wasps and bees

Wasps and bees inject
venom by stinging.
They sting with a
pointed tube.

You can see the
sharp stinging tube
on this wasp.

A sting is very painful.

Bees sting animals that attack their nests for
food. This hurts the animal. It runs away.

Some wasps sting to catch food for
their young.

A wasp stings a spider.
The venom makes the
spider stay very still.

The wasp drags the spider back
to its underground nest.
It lays an egg on
the spider.

The egg hatches out,
and the young wasp
eats the spider.

Stinging scorpions

Scorpions sting to kill animals for food.

A fattail scorpion hides in a crack in a rock. A cricket passes close by.

The scorpion grabs the cricket using its pincers, then holds the cricket still.

It injects venom into the cricket using the pointed stinging tube on its tail.

The venom flows into the cricket. The cricket dies and then the scorpion eats it.

Scorpions also sting to protect their babies.

This scorpion is carrying her babies on her back. Her stinging tail is curled over them.

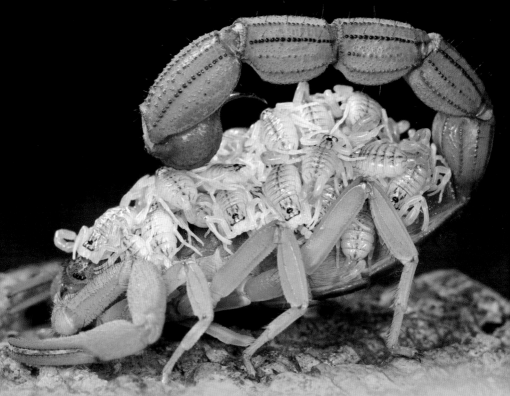

She'll sting any animals that come near.

The venom from some scorpions is so strong it could kill a person.

Dangerous caterpillars

Some caterpillars have poison in their bodies. Animals that eat or even touch the caterpillars may become very ill.

This is a swallowtail caterpillar.

Animals learn that these caterpillars are poisonous and stay away from them.

Other caterpillars have sharp, hollow spines that inject painful venom.

The spines on this saddleback caterpillar will inject venom into animals that attack it.

Some caterpillars are covered in long hairs.

The hairs on this pale tussock moth caterpillar make the skin and noses of animals itch.

Bad bugs

Some animals use venom to stop other animals from attacking them.

A hungry toad tries to grab a bombardier beetle to eat.

The beetle sprays boiling hot venom through a tube on its body.

The hot venom burns the toad's skin and makes it go away.

Assassin bugs spit venom into the eyes of animals that try to eat them.

They use venom to kill things, too. This bug has stuck its sharp mouth tube into a bee and is injecting venom.

The venom turns the bee's insides to liquid so the assassin bug can suck them out.

Danger at sea

Some sea creatures have venom that they use to attack animals for food, or to stop animals from attacking them.

A cone snail crawls along the seabed. It sees a fish it wants to eat.

A long tube shoots out of the snail's mouth. It injects venom into the fish.

The venom makes the fish stay still. The snail pulls the fish into its mouth.

A stingray is a big fish with a stinging tail that it uses to hurt attackers.

This is a lionfish. Each of its pointed fins is a stinging spine.

The spines will inject painful venom into anything that touches them.

Tentacles

Jellyfish are sea creatures with stinging tentacles that they use to kill fish.

This is a sea nettle jellyfish.

Fish swim into the long, thin tentacles.
Each tentacle injects venom into the fish.

The jellyfish uses its thick arms to push fish into its mouth.

An octopus has tentacles to catch food, too.

It uses its tentacles to grab a crab, then pushes the crab up to its mouth.

The octopus bites the crab. Venom in its spit flows into the crab and kills it.

Its tentacles tear the shell off the crab, then it eats the meat inside.

Warning signs

Some animals have markings to warn that they are poisonous.

This is a poison dart frog. It has powerful poison in its skin that will kill animals that try to eat it.

Its bright skin tells animals to stay away.

Some animals don't have poison or venom, but they look like animals that do. This stops them from being attacked.

Viceroy

Monarch

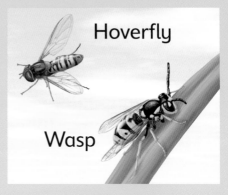

Hoverfly

Wasp

Viceroy butterflies look very similar to poisonous monarch butterflies.

A hoverfly is a type of fly. It looks like a wasp that stings.

Coral snake

Milk snake

Coral snakes inject venom when they bite. Milk snakes don't have any venom.

Other warnings

Other animals have different ways to show that they have poison or venom.

A blue-ringed octopus warns other animals not to attack by turning yellow with bright blue markings.

If it bites, it injects powerful venom.

A rattlesnake shakes its tail to make a rattling sound. This shows it has venom.

Before it bites, a wandering spider raises its legs and shows its red fangs.

A pufferfish has dangerous poison in its body. It swells up to warn other animals not to eat it.

Surprise poison

Some animals don't look as if they have poison or venom, but they do.

Water shrews have venom in their spit that they use to kill animals to eat.

This shrew is biting a worm. Venom will flow into the worm and kill it.

The pitohui bird has poisonous skin and feathers that stop other animals from eating it.

A male platypus has a sharp spike on its leg that injects venom. This may help the platypus to find a mate.

Two male platypuses see a female platypus.

The males fight. One male sticks his spike into the other.

Venom flows into the platypus and hurts it.

The male who is not hurt goes to join the female.

Glossary

Here are some of the words in this book you might not know. This page tells you what they mean.

 poison - a poisonous liquid that some animals have inside their bodies.

 venom - a poisonous liquid that one animal injects into another.

 sting - when an animal injects venom through a stinging tube.

 fangs - sharp, hollow teeth that some animals use to inject venom.

 spines - sharp spikes that inject venom into anything that touches them.

 markings - bright patches on an animal to show that it is poisonous.

 tentacles - long parts of a sea creature that it uses to sting or catch food.

Websites to visit

You can visit exciting websites to find out more about poisonous animals.

To visit these websites, go to the Usborne Quicklinks website at **www.usborne.com/quicklinks** Read the internet safety guidelines, and then type the keywords "**beginners poisonous animals**".

The websites are regularly reviewed and the links in Usborne Quicklinks are updated. However, Usborne Publishing is not responsible, and does not accept liability, for the content or availability of any website other than its own. We recommend that children are supervised while on the internet.

This milkweed locust's bright red body warns other animals that it is poisonous.

Index

Acknowledgements

Photographic manipulation by John Russell

Photo credits

The publishers are grateful to the following for permission to reproduce material:
cover © **Visuals Unlimited/naturepl.com**; p1© **Andy Teare/ardea.com**; p2-3 © **John Cancalosi/Alamy**; p4 © **Biosphoto/SuperStock**; p5 © **Minden Pictures/SuperStock**; p6 © **Stephen Dalton/naturepl.com**; p9 © **I love nature/Getty Images**; p10-11 © **Stephen Belcher/Minden Pictures/FLPA**; p12 © **Olivier Parent/Alamy**; p15 © **Ingo Arndt/Getty Images**; p16 © **Fabio Liverani/naturepl.com**; p17 © **Hagit Berkovich/Shutterstock** (saddleback caterpillar); © **blickwinkel/Alamy** (red-tail moth caterpillar); p19 © **Christian Musat/Alamy**; p21 © **Reinhard Dirscherl/Getty Images**; p22 © **Karen Doody/Stocktrek Images/Getty Images**; p24 © **Alfredo Maiquez/Getty Images**; p26 © **Alex Mustard/naturepl.com**; p28 © **Edo Schmidt/Alamy**; p31 © **Minden Pictures/SuperStock**.

Every effort has been made to trace and acknowledge ownership of copyright. If any rights have been omitted, the publishers offer to rectify this in any subsequent editions following notification.

 Sun, moon and stars

 Farm animals

 Elizabeth I

 Rubbish & Recycling

Dogs

 Horses and ponies

 Spiders

 Planes

Cats

 Ancient Greeks

 VOLCANOES

 DINOSAURS

 Your Body

 Armour

 Sharks

The Celts

 VIKINGS

 Castles

 How flowers grow

 Digging up the past

 Living in space

 Caterpillars and Butterflies

 Ballet

 Pirates

 EGYPTIANS

Eggs and Chicks

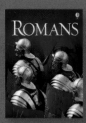
ROMANS

Weather

Tadpoles and Frogs

Why do we eat?

Under the Sea

Bears

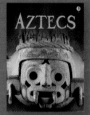
AZTECS

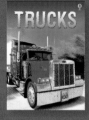
TRUCKS

Night Animals

Firefighters

Antarctica

Bugs

COWBOYS

Planet Earth

London

Seashore

China

Dangerous Animals

Rainforests

Trees

Reptiles

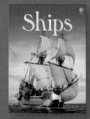
Ships

Bats

Penguins